Dogs

Christine Butterworth and Donna Bailey

Silver Burdett Press, Morristown, New Jersey

This is my dog.

His name is Chip.

I got him when he was a puppy.
Chip is the puppy on the left.

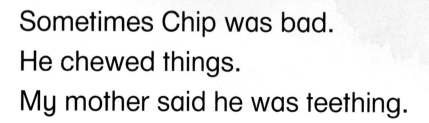

Sometimes Chip was bad.

He chewed things.

My mother said he was teething.

Puppies like to chew on things.
It helps their teeth grow.

My father said to train Chip.
Then I could take Chip for walks.

I trained Chip to walk near me.

I trained him to sit.

He will come when I call, too.

Now I walk Chip every day.
Dogs need to go for walks.
They need exercise.

8

I put Chip on his leash.

He stays near me.

He does not pull me.

He does not run into the street.

9

We play in the park often.

I throw a stick for Chip.

He brings it to me.

I feed Chip when we get home.

He runs a lot in the park.

Now he is very hungry.

I give Chip biscuits to chew.
I give him fresh water, too.

12

Sometimes I give Chip a bone to chew.
The bone keeps his teeth strong.

I brush Chip every day.
This keeps him clean.
It makes his coat shine.

14

Chip sleeps in a basket at night.
He wakes up if he hears a sound.

Chip barks at strangers.

My father says he is a good watchdog.

He tells us when people come
to the house.

Dogs are good pets.

Some are good watchdogs, too.

Other dogs have different jobs to do.

Some work with animals.

Others help save people.

Long ago people had dogs to hunt.
These dogs kept animals away from crops.

18

Now dogs still help people.
They hunt and do other things, too.

Some dogs work with animals.
They help herd sheep.

The shepherd whistles to the sheepdogs.
This tells them where to go.

The sheepdogs herd the sheep together.
They bring them down to their pens.

These dogs are helping to herd cattle.

Huskies are big and strong.
They pull sleds over the snow.

Greyhounds run very fast.
They race around a track.

Dogs have very good noses.

Some dogs help the police.

They help find lost people or things.

This dog is looking for people.

The people are trapped by an earthquake.

The dog sniffs to find the people.

This dog is looking for someone.
The person is buried under the snow.

Guide dogs are eyes for people
who cannot see.
They help blind people get around.

Guide dogs wear a harness.

The harness has a handle.

The handle helps the dogs to guide people.

These dogs take care of their owners.
They help their owners
to cross streets safely.

Dogs are often our friends.

Maybe you have a dog for a friend.

Reading consultant: Diana Bentley
Editorial consultant: Donna Bailey

Illustrated by Gill Tomblin
Picture research by Suzanne Williams
Designed by Richard Garratt Design

First published in 1988 by
Macmillan Children's Books,
a division of Macmillan Publishers Limited
4 Little Essex Street, London WC2R 3LF and Basingstoke

Published in the United States by
Silver Burdett Press, Morristown, New Jersey.

Printed in Hong Kong

Library of Congress Cataloging-in-Publication Data
Butterworth, Christine.
    Dogs.
    (My world——red series)
    Summary: A child discusses the care, feeding,
handling, and training of a pet dog. Also describes
ways that working dogs help people.
    1. Dogs——Juvenile literature.   [1. Dogs]
I. Tomblin, Gill, ill.   II. Title.   III. Series: Butterworth, Christine.
My world——red Series.
SF426.5.B88   1988   636.7   87-26313
ISBN 0-382-09549-9

All photographs by Peter Greenland except:
Cover: Bruce Coleman/Hans Reinhard
Allsport: 25 (Vandystadt)
Animal Photography: 22, 26 & 29 (Sally Anne Thompson), 23
    (R. Willbie)
The Bridgeman Art Library: 18 (Victoria and Albert Museum)
Bruce Coleman: 17 (Hans Reinhard), 19 (L. Lee Rue), 24
    (Nicholas De Vore), 32 (Jen & Des Bartlett)
Rex Features: 27
Spectrum Colour Library: 3 (Anne Cumbers)